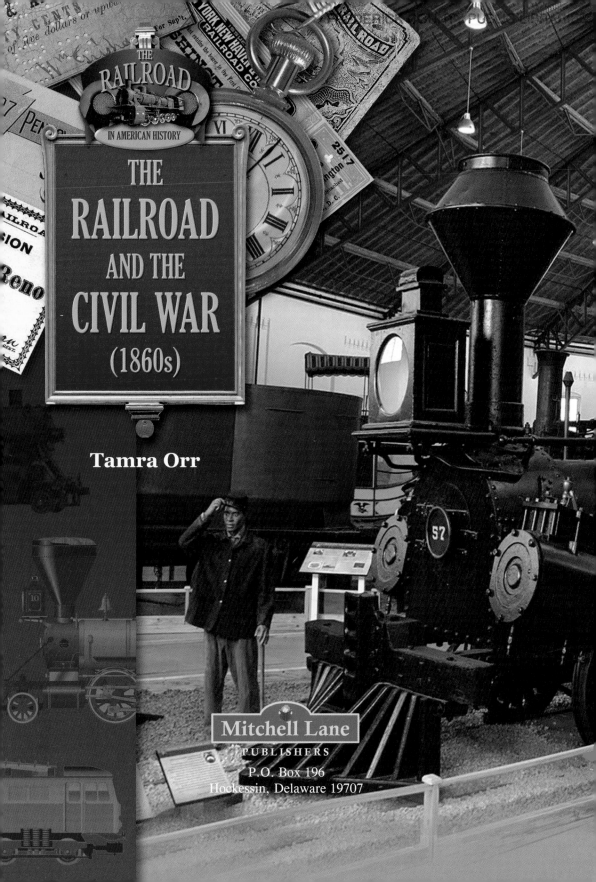

THE
RAILROAD
AND THE
CIVIL WAR
(1860s)

Tamra Orr

Mitchell Lane
PUBLISHERS
P.O. Box 196
Hockessin, Delaware 19707

THE RAILROAD

IN AMERICAN HISTORY

The Birth of the Locomotive
The Railroad Comes to America
The Railroad Grows into an Industry
The Railroad and the Civil War
The Railroad Fuels Westward Expansion
Electric Trains and Trolleys

The publisher would like to thank Milton C. Hallberg for acting as a consultant on its *The Railroad in American History* series. He is a professor emeritus of agricultural economics at Pennsylvania State University and has been a visiting professor at universities around the world. His railroad interests began when he attended a railroad telegraphers' school in preparation for a job as a depot agent on the CB&Q Railroad in Illinois. After retiring from teaching, he returned to his railroad interests as a new hobby, during which time he has written about early rail systems.

PUBLISHER'S NOTE:
      The facts on which this book is based have been thoroughly researched. Documentation of such research can be found on page 44. While every possible effort has been made to ensure accuracy, the publisher will not assume liability for damages caused by inaccuracies in the data, and makes no warranty on the accuracy of the information contained herein.

Printing
1   2   3   4   5   6   7   8   9

**Library of Congress
Cataloging-in-Publication Data**
Orr, Tamra.
 The railroad and the Civil War (1860s) / by Tamra Orr.
     p. cm. —(The railroad in American history)
 Includes bibliographical references and index.
 ISBN 978-1-61228-289-3 (library bound)
 1. Railroads—United States—History--19th century—Juvenile literature. 2. Railroads--United States—Design and construction—History—Juvenile literature. 3. United States—History—Civil War, 1861-1865--Transportation--Juvenile literature.
 I. Title.
 TF23.O77 2013
 385.0973'09034—dc23
                                            2012009427

eBook ISBN: 9781612283630

PLB

CONTENTS

"It is Done!"

When the final spike was driven into the railroad tie at 12:47 p.m. on May 10, 1869, at Promontory Summit in Utah, countless people cheered. Across the nation that Monday, the message was spread from one region to the next by telegraph message. "It is done!" it simply proclaimed. Church bells pealed! Cannons boomed and fireworks were lit in big cities. The Liberty Bell in Philadelphia rang out and local train whistles were sounded. After the nation's bitterly dividing Civil War, six years of incredibly hard and dangerous work, the labor of thousands of men, and millions of dollars spent, a railroad connecting one side of the country to the other was finally finished. It was one of the country's finest achievements and largest accomplishments. This triumph, however, did not come without a price—for some, a very high price.

Few people were thinking about that price when those precious spikes were put into the wooden railroad ties. Some were thinking about the huge profits they would continue to make or what businesses they might open. Others were

The transcontinental railroad is completed at Promontory Summit, Utah, on May 10, 1869.

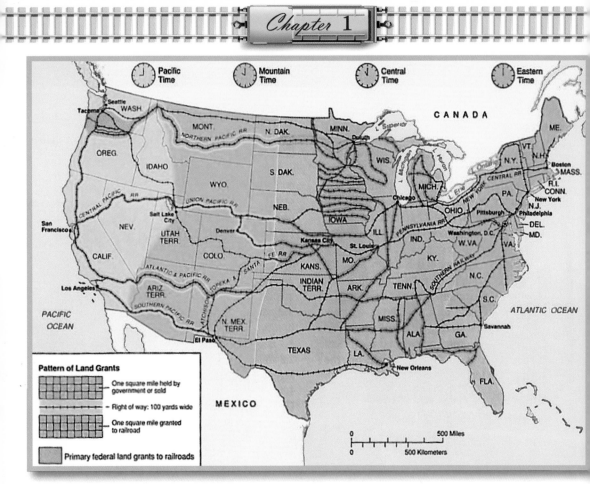

| Pacific Time | Mountain Time | Central Time | Eastern Time |

Transcontinental railroads and federal land grants, 1850–1900

Pattern of Land Grants
- One square mile held by government or sold
- Right of way: 100 yards wide
- One square mile granted to railroad
- Primary federal land grants to railroads

pondering how their lives would change now that they could travel, relocate, and explore the rest of the country. Many were just relieved that the grueling and dangerous physical work was finally over and they could go home.

The Special Spikes

On that amazing day in Utah, a crowd of 600 gathered to watch as the two rail lines, built from different directions for six years, met in the middle at last. The engines, *No. 119* and *Jupiter,* almost touched noses. Although newspaper reporters were there and many claimed to write eyewitness reports, in truth, they were pushed back so far by the eager crowd that hardly any of them could see what happened. Some even wrote their on-the-scene reports days after the event.

Because of the terrible view and the way information changes as it passes from one person to the next, many false stories were printed and then repeated over the years. Reporters wrote of a gleaming golden spike hammered into a standard wooden tie—but that didn't happen. Instead, a specially made railroad tie was prepared ahead of time, and four special spikes were hammered into it, but only for show. They were not left on the tracks.

As with national events, then and now, the ceremony began with speeches. A prayer was given, a banker spoke, and a newspaper editor droned on and on—and then finally, it was time to drive in the spikes. Few people knew that the wood tie measuring seven and a half feet (two and a quarter meters) and lying on the last rail section was not made of the traditional pine. Instead, it was made of a piece of highly polished and much softer laurel wood. Four holes had been drilled into the tie so when the special spikes were "driven in," they were actually being tapped into place. The tie had an engraved plaque on it listing the names of the officers and directors of the Central Pacific Railroad.

The first two spikes were tapped into the tie with a silver-plated maul held by Leland Stanford, president of the Central Pacific line. These spikes were certainly special. One was made by David Hewes, a friend of Stanford's. The spike was almost six inches (fifteen and a quarter centimeters) long and made of 17.6-karat gold. It had been engraved on all four sides and the top. Two sides had the names of railroad officers and directors. One side stated, "The Pacific Railroad ground broken Jany [sic January] 8th 1863 and completed May 8th 1869." Another side was engraved with, "May God continue the unity of our country as the railroad unites the two great Oceans of the world. Presented David Hewes San Francisco." The very top of the spike was engraved simply with, "The Last Spike."[1]

The second golden spike tapped in by Stanford had been made by the owner of a California newspaper. It was engraved, "With this spike the San Francisco News Letter offers its homage to the great work

Thomas Durant

which has joined the Atlantic and Pacific Oceans. This month-May, 1869."[2]

Next up to hold the maul was the Union Pacific's vice president, Thomas Durant. He was given a silver spike from Nevada and a mixed silver and gold spike from Arizona. The spikes were placed in their prepared holes and tapped into place. As people cheered and shouted, the valuable spikes and tie were removed. They were replaced with a pine tie, into which three ordinary iron spikes were driven. Now the fourth spike—the actual final one—was ready to be hammered in. This time, Stanford took a real swing—but he missed. Durant gave it a try, and also missed. A regular rail worker stepped in and finished the job of "wedding the two rails." The telegraph message was sent and the country rejoiced.

The transcontinental railroad linked the country together like nothing else could have. It opened up opportunities for people to move, cities to form, businesses to grow, and a nation to expand. It changed how people looked at their lives, their hopes, and their plans. At the same time, these train tracks changed the lives of many Native American tribes, driving innumerable families from their homelands and destroying much of the buffalo herds they had relied on all of their lives for survival.

Building the transcontinental railroad cost the lives of dozens of hard-working men, many of them immigrants who had hoped to find a better life in America. Instead, they found freezing temperatures, devastating blizzards, frightening explosions, and backbreaking work. The railroad was an accomplishment that astounded the nation and changed the lives of every citizen, in one way or another. The "wedding of the rails" was a moment in history that would never be forgotten for reasons of pride—and shame.

The War Between the States

Construction on the transcontinental railroad began while the American Civil War was raging between the North and the South. One of the biggest causes for the war was slavery.

The country was already divided over whether it was right to own human beings when Abraham Lincoln, a known opponent of slavery, was elected president in November 1860. By the time he took office in March 1861, South Carolina and six other Southern slave states had seceded from the union of the United States and formed the Confederate States of America.

The war's first shots were fired in April 1861, and soon four more Southern states joined the Confederacy. The brutal war pitted brothers against brothers, and friends against friends. In the midst of the turmoil, President Lincoln signed an act in July 1862 that allowed for the construction of a transcontinental railroad.

Slavery finally ended with the Thirteenth Amendment to the Constitution. It was passed by the Senate in April 1864 and by the House six months later. By the end of 1865, it was adopted when Georgia became the twenty-seventh state to ratify the amendment, giving it the required support of three-fourths of the states.

Lincoln had pushed hard for the amendment's passage, but he didn't live to see it take effect and free almost a million slaves. He was assassinated days after the Civil War drew to a close. On April 14, 1865, John Wilkes Booth snuck up behind Lincoln, who was sitting in a theater watching a play, and shot the President in the head. Lincoln died early the next morning.

CHAPTER 2

Which Route is Best?

There was no question the nation needed a transcontinental railroad, but which route was the best one to take? Deciding was difficult—it depended on how much it would cost, what type of land it would cross, how many workers it would require—and what effect the war would have. The growing conflict between the Union and Confederate regions of the country played a big role in where the tracks would be laid and what territory was covered. Each side was well aware of how important the railroad was in getting men and supplies where they needed to be. The North wanted a northern route; the South fought for a southern one.

Teams of surveyors were sent out and asked to settle the debate: Which route was the wisest to take? In 1854, the results were in. Jefferson Davis, the nation's Secretary of War, read over the recommendations and decided that the southern route made the most sense. Of course, he was not unbiased. He clearly favored the South. In fact, he later

This train is a replica of the original *Leviathan* that was built in 1868 by the Central Pacific Railroad.

Jefferson Davis was unable to avoid his personal bias when deciding on a route for the transcontinental railroad. General Robert E. Lee (center), who fought for the Confederacy in the Civil War, also struggled with the idea of a railroad that did not benefit the South.

became the president of the Confederate States of America. His decision was tossed out and everyone went back to waiting and wondering what would happen next.

Seven years later, all of the Southern representatives left Congress as they prepared to create their own separate country. The moment that happened, money was sent to start the construction of the railroad along a northern route.

"Crazy Judah" Forges Ahead

The idea for a train that traveled across the constantly growing country was not a new one. It had been discussed and debated for decades by some of the most creative and intelligent minds. There was no doubt that the transcontinental railroad was needed. Rail travel was clearly faster and more direct than going by wagon or water. What was far less clear, however, was how to do it. One look across the country was enough to intimidate anyone. Between one coast and the other were a lot of very tall, very solid mountain ranges. Many of their peaks were more than 14,000 feet (4,270 meters) tall. How would a train get over or around these towering structures?

One of the first people to seriously consider a train that could cross the United States was Asa Whitney. The idea came to him through a series of tragedies. His import business failed, he lost his house, and then his second wife died during childbirth. Desperate for a fresh start, Whitney moved to China where he started a successful business as a trader. Once he had money, he decided to return to America where he was determined to find a way to help people.

It became Whitney's mission to create a transcontinental railroad. In 1845, he asked the government for the land to get started. Congress did not say yes or no, but instead said they would think about it for a while. Unfortunately, Whitney was not a patient person. While Congress took its time deciding, he traveled all over the country speaking to groups of people and giving newspaper interviews in order to drum up support for his mission. His plan was bold, but it didn't work. In 1851, Congress finally told him no. Although other people went on to succeed where Whitney had failed, it was his passion for the idea that grabbed the nation's attention and helped pave the way for others to accomplish his dream.

Between 1848 and 1855, the lure of discovering gold brought thousands of settlers into the West. It was not an easy trip, taking weeks or even months, depending on the time of the year. Wagon trains moved slowly, and often had to navigate around high mountain ranges, raging rivers, and angry Native American tribes defending their territory. Accidents were common, from being run over by wagon wheels or stampeding livestock to suffering from firearm injuries. Illness was also a common risk and cholera, a dangerous and highly contagious disease, would sometimes rush through an entire group of travelers and leave no survivors. Clearly, this long trip was full of danger and difficulty and people were eager for a better way to make the journey. They already knew that trains were a faster, easier way to travel and the push to create a train that would go west grew quickly, but the same question remained: How could it be done? Which path was the best one to take?

Throughout the decade, a number of inventive men came up with possible pathways. They took their ideas to Congress and the president and asked for the support and money to start construction. An engineer named Theodore Judah finally won the battle for the best route. Judah was so knowledgeable and passionate about trains that he had earned the nickname "Crazy Judah".[1] He had helped build the Sacramento Valley Line, one of the first railroads west of the Missouri River.

Judah's plan was different in two ways. First, he felt that it would take businessmen to build the train system, rather than government. Second, he figured out a route across the Sierra Nevada Mountains in California that would only require one steep climb at Donner Pass. This was a definite improvement over other plans that had included two challenging climbs.

It was not long before Judah had the financial support he needed from businessman Collis Huntington and his associates, known as the Big Four.

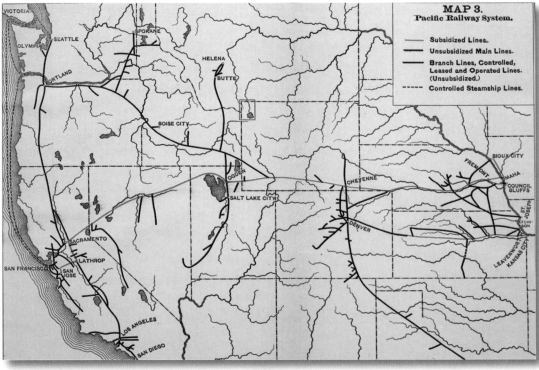

Early Pacific Railroad map

Lincoln's Pacific Railway Act brought jobs to many parts of the nation, and created countless towns and cities where before there was nothing but wilderness.

Now that he had money and a map, Judah was ready to get started. When President Abraham Lincoln signed the Pacific Railroad Act in July 1862, Judah knew he was sure to succeed, despite the fact that the nation was in the middle of a Civil War. The act stated that the American government would give large amounts of land—millions of acres—throughout the West to two companies in order to create a transcontinental railroad. It also guaranteed enormous amounts of money, since a project this size was beyond the ability of any single business or organization to fund. The Central Pacific Railroad would

Theodore Judah was a man obsessed with creating a transcontinental railroad. His passion was so strong that some people saw him as crazy. His sponsors found him exasperating!

build east from Sacramento, California. The Union Pacific would build west from Omaha, Nebraska. The two would meet in Utah.

Although the plans for the rail system kept moving forward, Judah's part in the project began to change. He started arguing with the Big Four. He often had different opinions about what to do and how to do it. Soon, tension between the men escalated. The Big Four made decisions without telling Judah. He grew angry and frustrated and finally decided to find other investors. Before that could happen, Judah got sick and died.

On January 8, 1863, the Central Pacific side held its groundbreaking ceremony in Sacramento, California. The first shovel of dirt was dug by none other than the newly elected governor, Leland Stanford. The Union Pacific side took much longer to get started, with its groundbreaking ceremony held on December 2, 1863, in Omaha, Nebraska.

Progress on each side was slow in the beginning. The Central Pacific only cleared about twenty miles (thirty-two kilometers) in the first few years of construction. One reason was that the cost of materials was skyrocketing, thanks to the Civil War. Steel, for example, went from $55 a ton to more than $115 a ton once the war started. Not only were supplies more expensive, they were harder and harder to obtain. Would this transcontinental railroad project fall apart before it was finished?

The Big Four Businessmen

Charles Crocker

Charles Crocker (1822–1885) spent years in a number of businesses before becoming part of the railroad. He went from being a miner to a merchant, and was involved in politics when fellow businessman Collis Huntington asked him to join him in building a railroad.

Crocker's construction company was given the first contract, which he quickly subcontracted to other companies since he had little idea of what he was doing. He learned quickly, however, and would prove to be one of the most innovative thinkers of all.

Mark Hopkins (1813–1878) headed west in search of gold, but ended up opening a grocery store with partner Collis Huntington. He had a great mind for numbers and was in charge of accounting and bookkeeping. When he and Huntington entered the railroad business, his talent for math was helpful as he handled massive amounts of money—and not always in the most honest ways. When he was caught in a scandal with some of the money, he actually burned his record books.

Collis Huntington (1821–1900) was a smart businessman who knew just what products to sell to make a profit. He was fascinated by Theodore Judah's train plans and soon invested a great deal of his money and time in the Central Pacific end of the project. It was a good decision since the railroad made him extremely wealthy. Huntington's ethics were not always the best—he often cheated and lied, but he was still a rich and respected tycoon.

Leland Stanford (1824–1893) was a Central Pacific investor, as well as a successful grocery store owner. He knew how to persuade crowds and keep people calm and was often sent to talk to upset investors, workers, and politicians. Stanford was the one who was supposed to hammer in the final iron spike when the rails were finished, but history says he missed and hit the tie instead. Today he is still known as the founder of one of the most prestigious colleges in the country, Stanford University in California.

CHAPTER 3

North Versus South

The construction of the new railroad was an exciting step for the country, but it didn't grab the biggest headlines. Instead, the news that filled the front pages was about the ongoing Civil War (1861–1865). The battle between the northern states and the southern states was fought over many issues, including slavery. It is remarkable that a war that divided the country was happening at the same time that a railroad was being built to unite the same country. Although the war slowed down construction and made the cost of supplies soar, it was not enough to stop this amazing accomplishment.

Trains were extraordinarily important to the Civil War. The railroad was still young, and it played a huge role in this national battle. In the previous twenty years, more than a hundred small train companies had been developed by private companies, as well as a few state governments. Until the war, these trains had been mainly used for moving cargo and equipment.

U.S. military engine *Firefly*
crosses a bridge

Before the transcontinental railroad was built, many small trains traveled short distances, moving cargo and livestock through stations like this one at Hanover Junction in Pennsylvania.

Now, many of these trains sent troops whatever they needed on the battlefield. They brought reinforcements when more soldiers were needed. They whisked soldiers out of dangerous areas when enemy troops grew too close or threatened to overtake them. These trains kept lines of communication open between commanders and troops, making it possible to send battle plans down the line. They brought in more weapons, which took hours instead of days to arrive. Trains carried food to hungry soldiers and medical supplies to the wounded. They transported the seriously injured to hospitals, and some trains were even hospitals on wheels, complete with doctors and nurses and beds for the patients.

One of the most unusual ways the trains were used during this time in history was to transport large hot air balloons. First, the men would inflate these balloons, usually with coal gas. Then the balloon would be secured to a flat cargo car on the train. During the journey, soldiers had to watch and make sure the balloon wasn't going to be pierced by a low-hanging branch or other sharp object. Once the train arrived in the battle area, the balloon was released. A soldier was tied to the balloon so that he could rise above the battleground and report the location of enemy troops and any other helpful information. Strong men would pull the rope and bring the spy and his balloon back to the ground.

Of course, because rail lines were such an important connection for troops, the rail lines were also targeted for attacks. Ambushes by both sides were quite common. Trains were sabotaged, tracks were torn up, and stations were burned down by the North and the South. Confederate and Union troops placed heavy obstacles on the tracks to prevent passage, or removed ties and set them on fire so they couldn't be used again to make repairs.

Some men even stayed long enough to heat the iron and twist it around trees, creating what came to be known as "Sherman hairpins," named after General William T. Sherman, head of the Union Army.[1] Wooden bridges were set on fire or brought down with simple pipe bombs. Other bridges were weakened so they would collapse under the weight of a moving train.

Sometimes handcars were used to send messages or important supplies to troops. The handcars took a lot of hard physical work, but they were simple to use and faster than being on foot. These handcars were also used to move wounded soldiers, to warn trains of danger on the tracks, and even to transport important officers from one place to the next, especially at night when trains could not see well enough to travel safely in the dark.

The Civil War finally came to an end on April 9, 1865 with the surrender of the South side's popular leader, General Robert E. Lee. He signed the terms at the Appomattox Court House in Virginia with the victorious Northern leader General Ulysses S. Grant. It was not an easy defeat for Lee. He stated, "There is nothing for me left to do but to go and see General Grant, and I would rather die a thousand deaths."[2]

By the time the war ended, more than 620,000 men had died, either in battle or from disease. The nation was united, but still wounded. The transcontinental railroad was a way to help heal that terrible wound. It worked as a way to join one side of the country with the other through thousands of miles of railroad tracks. In doing so, many had hopes that it would also help people—those in the North and the South—to feel as one—simply as Americans.

Changes Come Along the Rails

Without a doubt, the creation of railroads changed America. The ability to quickly travel and explore from coast to coast helped people create cities and states. The railroad built huge businesses. It was the key to finding out what this vast country had to offer and what adventures and opportunities were waiting for anyone brave enough to discover them. The huge accomplishment was not without victims, however. One of the largest groups of people damaged by the nation's rail system was Native Americans.

Long before any railroad tracks were laid, before Crazy Judah or other explorers had come through the area and scouted it for the best route, the Plains Indians had been living throughout the western part of the country. The horses brought to the area by earlier Spanish explorers had helped the tribes move into this portion of the nation and so, for more than a century, they had raised their children, hunted for food, and planted crops in this region. That all changed when the railroads came through. Suddenly hundreds of people flooded the area to build the rails and to work in the cities that formed along the tracks. They not only pushed the Native Americans out of their homeland, but they also hunted buffalo at such a huge rate that the millions that had roamed the area were reduced to less than a thousand by the end of the century. Many tribes depended heavily on the buffalo herds for food, and the destruction of this animal forced them to move or starve. They found ways to fight back, of course. Some attacked work crews

The arrival of the transcontinental railroad destroyed the lives of many Native American tribes, and also brought an end to the plentiful buffalo herds that had helped keep these tribes alive for so many generations.

and some destroyed the tracks. Some found ways to derail trains and others set up blockades on the rails.

When the Native Americans refused to leave their lands and tried to interfere with the construction of the train tracks, the United States sent in troops. In the fall of 1864, the tension that was growing between Native Americans and the army exploded. Hundreds of Cheyenne Indians were spending the winter in an area of Colorado called Sand Creek. Even though they had been invited to stay there by the U.S. Army, a restless and angry officer named Colonel John Chivington was tired of dealing with reluctant Native Americans. During the dark hours of the night, he and his men went to Sand Creek. As the sun rose that morning, Chivington uttered the order, "Kill and scalp all, big and little; nits make lice."[3] Even though Chief Black Kettle held up the white flag of surrender, Chivington's men did not stop. When the day was over, more than 150 Cheyenne had been killed, many of them women and children.

Although this photo shows Colonel Chivington sitting comfortably with Black Kettle and his men, it would not be long before they were all engaged in a battle to the death. By the time the fighting ended, hundreds were killed.

Revenge was swift. Six weeks later, a thousand Sioux, Arapaho, and Cheyenne razed the town of Julesburg, Colorado. They killed many people, burning the town behind them. They also tore down train stations and telegraph wires. Army troops followed, killing nearly 200 Arapaho who had had nothing to do with the attack. The people who worked on the rails were understandably frightened of what newspapers, politicians, and others had taken to calling the "Indian Menace." This situation only got worse when army troops moved into the Bozeman Trail, a sacred hunting ground for many tribes. A group of Plains Indians tricked some of the army into the forest and soon, every one of the soldiers was dead.

For the Native Americans, this was the beginning of what would become a steady loss. The railroad kept growing, settlers kept flooding into the region, towns kept forming, buffalo kept being slaughtered, and eventually it added up to mean that the Native American way of life would change in many ways.

Attack of the Rails

Colonel Thomas "Stonewall" Jackson

It is no surprise that railroad tracks often became the site of some of the Civil War's most fierce battles. These tracks were so helpful in transporting supplies and men to where they were needed that stopping cargo from reaching its destination or, even better, damaging the tracks so trains couldn't be used, became an effective battle strategy.

One of the largest battles took place in the spring of 1861 on the Baltimore and Ohio Railroad, better known as the B&O. Every day, train cars filled with coal destined for Union navy ships traveled to the North. To reach the North, however, the train had to travel though Virginia and West Virginia—two states fighting on the Southern side of the war.

That spring, Colonel Thomas Jackson put a plan into action. Earlier, he had complained to the railroad company that the constant train traffic was making it impossible for his tired soldiers to get any rest. He asked that trains be restricted to traveling between 11 A.M. and 1 P.M. The B&O agreed—and soon there was a backlog of more than fifty trains with hundreds of cars on the tracks during those two hours.

On May 23, trains were stacked up for miles, waiting their turn on the track, and Jackson attacked. He and his troops moved in and took control of the train cars. They hitched ten of the engines to powerful horses and pulled them away to Southern train tracks. Then they destroyed train tracks and bridges. Some coal cars were set on fire and others were hidden inside barns and on farms. Soon more than one hundred miles (160 kilometers) of tracks were under the control of the Confederate forces. It took B&O months of work and countless dollars to repair the damage.

CHAPTER 4

Finding the Workers

Even today it is hard to imagine how truly difficult it was to build the transcontinental railroad. Hundreds of miles of tracks and ties had to be laid down. Much of it was supposed to cross solid mountains with peaks that soared into the clouds. How could it possibly be done? Tunnels seemed to be the best option, but what could break through miles of hard granite?

Even harder was the weather that had to be endured during the construction. During the winter of 1866–1867, forty-four storms tore through the construction area. Huge snowdrifts blew in and closed tunnel entrances. Many workers had to use their shovels to dig through the snow and open the entrances again. Before the railroad was done, men saw raging blizzards that left them working in snow up to their waists. They endured freezing temperatures and terrifying avalanches that created even more danger than

Workers on the Pacific
Railroad battle a snowdrift

the explosives they used. A job building the railroad was not for the cowardly or the weak.

As the Central Pacific team of workers began slowly making their way east from California, the Union Pacific team lagged behind. They started months later for one simple reason: they could not find enough men to work for them. As chief engineer Peter Dey wrote to Thomas Durant, "It is impossible to do anything in the way of letting this work now without some provision for furnishing men."[1] Many men were still fighting on the battlegrounds of the Civil War. Others had been injured and were still recovering. Durant tried finding additional men by asking the government for some of the slaves that had been recently freed, but was denied. It was not until the war finally ended that the team found enough workers. Suddenly, thousands of soldiers were available, along with a number of Irishmen who had come to America to escape the terrible Potato Famine that had led to poverty and starvation in their homeland.

In spring 1868, another group of laborers joined this team. These men were Mormons from Utah. The region had been attacked by a horde of grasshoppers and many of the crops had been completely destroyed. With nothing to plant or harvest and no money coming in for their crops, these farmers needed to earn money doing something else—just when the Union Pacific needed more men to make the final push into Utah. In an interview with KUED-TV, author David Haward Bain stated, "And so it was done through a community and a church organization, and all of the farmers who really had absolutely nothing to do at that point, because of the fact that they'd lost all their crops, just poured down from the hillsides to take advantage of this. Bringing their plows, bringing their teams of horses, and ready to show up for a good day's work."[2]

Although the Central Pacific team had gotten a head start when it moved east from California, it had the same problem as the other team—far more work to do than workers to do it. Many of their men were Irish immigrants, but there were not enough of them. They would

A caravan of covered wagons carrying Mormons in search of work became a familiar sight in 1879. Their search often ended with long and difficult jobs building the railroad.

sometimes pass the time by singing and their songs gave clues to how hard the work was. One popular song stated,

> "When I lay me down to sleep
> The ugly bugs around me creep.
> Bad luck to wink that I can sleep,
> While workin' on the railroad."[3]

Railroad work was so physically exhausting that holding on to labor was difficult. Many men left their jobs to be part of the country's hunt for gold. Finally, in frustration at how slowly the team was moving, Crocker suggested a new idea. Why not hire some of the 60,000 Chinese immigrants who had come to the California area in recent years in search of work? Like many others, the Chinese came to America hoping to find anything from a job to a fortune in gold. Even as far away as

China, people had heard the convincing call of the Gold Rush and answered it by crossing the ocean to an unfamiliar land and dangerous jobs extracting metals, building irrigation systems, working in factories—and constructing a national railroad.

The group decided to hire a few Chinese men to see what would happen. Would the competition help keep the Irishmen from leaving their jobs? Soon the answer to that question didn't matter, as the leaders for the Central Pacific discovered something they had never expected: the Chinese, sometimes referred to as "Celestials" due to their religious beliefs, were amazing workers. They asked for less money than the Irish, often took care of their own cooking, always showed up for work, were quiet and clean, and were exceptionally careful.

In June 1867, the Chinese did something no one expected—they went on strike. They wanted what many workers want—higher pay,

The Chinese workers were one of the best things to happen to the transcontinental railroad. They were incredibly dedicated workers and proved to be a key factor in the tracks being finished on time. Despite this, they were often treated very poorly.

fewer hours, and shorter shifts. Crocker refused to meet a single one of their demands and instead, he withheld their food for a week. Finally, the Chinese gave in and returned to work having gained nothing.

Within a year, thousands of Chinese were employed by the railroad and by the end of the project, 80 percent of the workers on the Central Pacific were Chinese.[4] Crocker later stated, "Wherever we put them, we found them good, and they worked themselves into our favor to such an extent that if we found we were in a hurry for a job of work, it was better to put Chinese on at once."[5] Despite all of this, when that final celebration photo was taken at Promontory Summit in Utah, not a single Chinese worker could be seen.

From One to the Next
None of the work done on the transcontinental railroad was easy. It was intense, challenging, physical work that took a combination of muscles, skills, and patience. Using simple tools like shovels, saws, sledgehammers, and pick axes, plus wheelbarrows and plows pulled by oxen or horses, these men managed to cut down trees, blast through rocks, build bridges, and dig countless tons of dirt.

Each man on the team had a specific role and job to do. After surveyors had mapped the area for the tracks to be laid, graders came in to clear the region of rocks and trees and make sure the ground was fairly level. Next, men unloaded the long wooden rails and put them into place. Gaugers measured to see that the rails were exactly where they were supposed to be, and bolters joined the rails loosely. Spike men walked along the rails dropping spikes on the ground next to the rails, and these were picked up by hammer-wielders who used powerful swings of the sledgehammer to drive the spikes firmly into the ties. In addition to these men, there were special teams that built trestles and bridges.

Without a doubt, one of the toughest obstacles both teams faced was tunneling through mountain ranges, especially the dozen tunnels through the Sierra Nevada. Not only was the work slow, it was also very dangerous. Often a team would progress less than two feet (half a meter) a day. In some tunnels, workers drilled from several ends at once. The debris created by all of the tunneling had to be carted out. It was a backbreaking job. The men worked in three shifts of eight hours each, around the clock.

Workers relied primarily on black powder for their explosions. It did not take long before Crocker and other leaders discovered that the Chinese were unusually skilled at this process. When the Chinese had to blast through Cape Horn, they requested that some reeds from nearby marshes be brought to them. They used them to weave waist-high baskets. Next, they climbed into the baskets and then had other workers lower them down the side of the mountain by ropes. From the baskets, the Chinese drilled holes in the rock, inserted the black powder, lit the fuse, and then yelled to be pulled up before the explosion. It became one of the most effective ways to get through the tunnel.

Workers would light fuses to detonate nitroglycerin (or black powder) placed inside drilled holes in the rock.

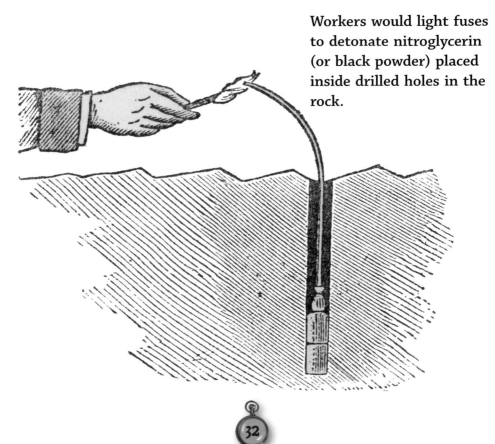

In 1866, a different way to blast through the mountains was used. Nitroglycerin had been discovered a few years earlier by a chemist and Crocker wanted to test the compound on tunnels. Before he could learn anything, a shipment of nitro, as it was called, exploded accidentally in San Francisco, leveling buildings, killing more than a dozen people, and scaring the entire city. A smaller amount also exploded unexpectedly at the Central Pacific rail line, killing six workers. In a panic, the state of California banned all nitro shipments. Crocker was frustrated.

His problem was solved a year later when James Howden, a British chemist, came to him and told him he could make nitro for him. Crocker decided to risk it and it was the right decision. Howden's nitro was incredibly successful. It worked in wet rock, used shallower holes, was easier to clean up and, most importantly, went through rock unbelievably fast. Suddenly, progress sped up. Instead of moving less than two feet (half a meter) a day, the teams were tunneling more than twice as far. Although it was far better than black powder, nitroglycerin was also extremely dangerous, so when the Summit Tunnel was finished, Crocker went back to black powder.

The workers behind the building of the transcontinental railroad ranged from the Irish and Chinese to former Civil War soldiers and out-of-work Mormons. All of them played an important role in creating one of the biggest systems of transportation in the world.

Chugging Along

Although the transcontinental railroad being laid across the country was new, trains themselves were not. They had been chugging across tracks in different parts of the country years before the Civil War started. By 1830, there were only about twenty-three miles (thirty-seven kilometers) of railroad in the United States. By 1850, that number had grown to about 9,000 miles (14,500 kilometers). President Millard Fillmore signed the first Railroad Land Grant Act, encouraging railroad companies to form and begin building in undeveloped areas of the

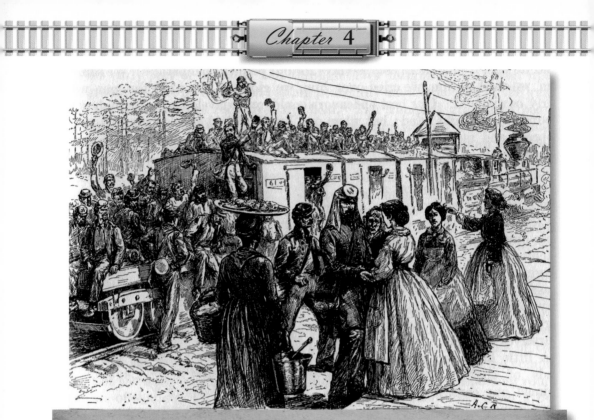

Even before the transcontinental railroad was completed, people relied on trains. Soldiers would often be taken to the war from some of the smaller stations.

nation. By the time the Civil War began, there was more than 30,000 miles (48,280 kilometers) of rails throughout the United States.

As more tracks were built and more people began to depend on trains, the locomotives themselves went through quite a few changes also. The very first trains were pulled by horses, but by the 1830s, they were moved with steam power. Locomotives got bigger and faster. By the time the trains were called on to help both sides of the country during the Civil War, they had knuckle couplers, mechanisms that connected one car to the next, and air brakes.

An Ode to the Rails

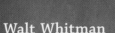

Walt Whitman

One place people's passion and excitement about the railroad was evident was in the poetry being published at the time. Ralph Waldo Emerson called the train " . . . the Iron Horse, the earth-shaker, the fire-breather . . . "[6] and Walt Whitman, in his poem "Song of Joys," wrote, "O the engineer's joys! To go with a locomotive! To hear the hiss of steam, the merry shriek, the steam-whistle, the laughing locomotive! To push with resistless way and speed off in the distance."[7] Poet Francis Bret Harte wrote in "What the Engines Said" about the opening of the railroad in Utah, "What was it the engines said, Pilots touching,—head to head, Facing on the single track, Half a world behind each back? . . . How two Engines—in their vision—Once have met without collision. . . . With a whistle at the close."[8]

Although the poets made the railroad sound wonderful, the reality was that it was also amazingly difficult and dangerous to build. How many people lost their lives in the process is a question no one can answer with certainty. Some newspaper articles of the time claimed it was thousands, but actual numbers are most likely much smaller. Surprisingly enough, of the several hundred people who died, most succumbed to either weather-related events such as blizzards and avalanches or to diseases such as smallpox. Experts believe that fewer than forty people actually died in construction accidents.

On to Promontory Summit!

After six years, the end of the transcontinental railroad was in sight. As hard as it had been for everyone, the project was still coming in almost seven years ahead of schedule. As the two teams got closer and closer, a rivalry developed between them. Who would reach Utah first? It was not just a question of pride. The rail line that reached the state first would be assured of the majority of the money, land, and profit. Whichever track got through Weber Canyon, not far from Ogden, Utah, would be able to claim its rich coalmines. Winning not only meant more attention and pride—it meant more wealth and power.

Union Pacific executive Thomas Durant nudged Central Pacific executive Leland Stanford with a telegram when his team got past the Rocky Mountains. It was a polite way to say, "I'm winning!" In April 1869, Crocker pushed this competition even further. He made a bet with Durant on which team could put down the most miles of track in a single day. Crocker's team won, laying an astounding ten

The *No. 119* meets the *Jupiter*
in this re-creation.

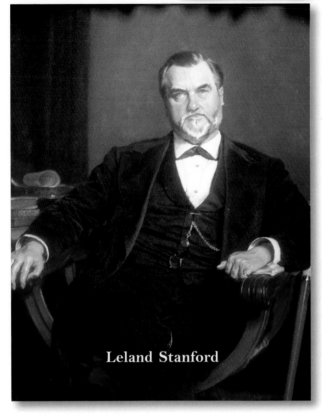

Leland Stanford

miles (sixteen kilometers) of track between sunrise and sunset and winning the $10,000 bet.

As the race sped up and the pressure increased, the work the men were doing got sloppier and sloppier. Running low on funds, the men tried to stretch their materials and supplies. They worked to put down the tracks as fast as humanly possible—even if that meant they weren't doing it safely. Although it would not be discovered for several years after the big celebration at Promontory Summit, some of the work done in these final weeks was so badly constructed that hundreds of miles had to be redone and paid for by taxpayers. Trestles collapsed, and curves built at the wrong angles were taken dangerously fast by the trains. Everything had to be replaced.

The meeting point of Promontory Summit (often mistakenly called Promontory Point by reporters at the time and repeated incorrectly ever since) in Utah was an agreement between the Union Pacific and the Central Pacific. However, it took months of bickering and discussion, plus a number of meetings, and even pressure from Congress before the exact spot was chosen.

Even the time of the meeting ran into some problems. The original date was supposed to be May 8, but on their way to Utah, Durant and other officials from the Union Pacific were delayed. Why? Hundreds of workers who had not been paid by the railroad company blocked the train tracks and demanded payment. When Durant refused, the men uncoupled his train car. It was moved to a sidetrack and chained. Durant was told to send for the $80,000 owed to the men. When he refused one more time, they threatened to take him up into the mountains and hold him hostage. Finally, money was sent, the men were paid, and another engine took the officials on to the waiting celebration at Promontory Summit.[1]

Not long after the transcontinental railroad was finished, the sloppiness of some of the work and the need for replacement slowly became obvious. That was followed by new information as the years passed.

In 1872, a scandal surfaced showing that Durant had bought an accounting company and made it appear to be a construction company called Credit Mobilier. Then he made sure that the Union Pacific Railroad, where he was vice president, awarded the contract to build the railroad to Credit Mobilier. In essence, this meant that Durant could not lose. He would make money no matter what happened, even if it was not legal or fair. He and other investors kept most of the money, paying less to other construction crews to do the work. Durant made millions of dollars in profit through this less than ethical arrangement. Even though it was discovered, no charges were pressed and no one was ever punished.

Another black mark that is associated with the transcontinental railroad occurred ten years later. Despite the fact that the railroad would never have been completed without the help of the Chinese, in 1882, Congress passed the Chinese Exclusion Act. This act banned any Chinese workers from coming into the United States for ten years. Americans were unhappy that so many of the Chinese were competing for the limited number of available jobs. As time passed, tension between the two groups grew higher, resulting in the act that limited Chinese from coming to America. When those ten years were over, Congress extended the act—and then did it again in 1904.

A Different World

When the two sides of the United States were finally connected, the effects were felt in endless ways. The feeling of unity helped to heal a nation still recovering from the pain and losses of the Civil War. The country also seemed somehow closer, because it did not take a life-threatening journey of weeks or even months to cross it. Now the trip could be made in about a week's time and at a fraction of the cost.

The trading industry was monumentally changed. Goods and services could be sent from one side of the country to the other, and soon millions of dollars of freight was going back and forth every year. Words printed in the East were read in the West—and vice versa, opening up people's minds to new ideas and concepts. Families now had ways to get a new start in a new land. Adventurers had exotic places to explore, and entrepreneurs had many different businesses to open in newly created cities along the train routes.

The transcontinental railroad also inspired other train companies and routes to develop. Soon tracks were laid in all directions, allowing people to travel and settle wherever their imaginations led them. Other countries were motivated. Train systems developed in places such as Canada, Asia, and Africa.

These hundreds of miles of tracks changed the way Americans lived, worked, and thought, even though they also tragically changed the lives of countless Native Americans. Today, trains still cross the country, although they tend to carry more cargo than they do passengers. The sound of a train whistle, the rumble of its engine, and the rhythm of its wheels turning on the tracks is still enough to inspire people to want to pack their bags, buy their tickets, and then travel and explore. New horizons beckon in the simply stated invitation of, "All aboard!" Those two words embody the incredible dreams and hard work of all of the people who helped to build the transcontinental railroad.

The Harvey Girls

Long before you could hop off a train and find a row of coffee shops, snack bars, and restaurants waiting to fill you up, there was little for the early railroad passengers to eat and drink. The companies that did offer such fare often charged ridiculously high prices for low quality food. A man named Fred Harvey thought something had to be done to improve this situation, so in the mid-1870s, he created the Harvey House, a chain of restaurants along the Santa Fe line. The first one opened in 1876 and at its peak, there were eighty-four Harvey Houses along the rail route.

Good food at a reasonable price was popular—but what made the chain even more popular was its servers, known as the Harvey Girls. These young women came from all over the country in response to newspaper ads requesting attractive girls between the ages of eighteen and thirty who had strong morals, a good education, and excellent manners. Once the girls were hired, they had to promise not to get married for at least six months. This was difficult since pretty, young women were often in short supply in these parts of the country and marriage proposals arrived faster than food orders! The girls wore long black-and-white uniforms that covered up as much as possible and each one of them was interviewed by Harvey's wife before being hired.

A movie was made about these young women in 1946. "The Harvey Girls" starred Judy Garland and Angela Lansbury. The Harvey Company operated restaurants throughout the country until the late 1960s, when it was purchased by another company. As many as 100,000 young women became Harvey Girls and one railroad man was quoted as calling the restaurants, "the Cupid of the Rails."[2]

1860 Theodore Judah realizes the Donner Pass is a perfect place to build the railroad.

1861 The Civil War begins.

1862 President Abraham Lincoln signs the Pacific Railway Act authorizing the transcontinental railroad. Judah plans to build the railroad across the Sierra Nevada Mountains. The Central Pacific Railroad is financed by the Big Four.

1863 The first load of dirt is shoveled at the Central Pacific groundbreaking ceremony. The first spike is hammered into the ties. Judah dies.

1864 Congress passes a revised Pacific Railroad Bill. The Sand Creek Massacre is carried out.

1865 The railroad companies begin using Chinese workers. The Civil War ends. President Lincoln is assassinated.

1867 The Chinese go on strike for one week before returning to work.

1869 The Central Pacific and Union Pacific meet at Promontory Summit in Utah.

1872 The Credit Mobilier scandal is revealed.

1882 The Chinese Exclusion Act is passed and then renewed in 1892 and 1904.

CHAPTER NOTES

Chapter 1. "It is Done!"
1. National Park Service, "Golden Spike: Four Special Spikes,"
   http://www.nps.gov/gosp/historyculture/upload/Spikes.pdf
2. Ibid.

Chapter 2. Which Route is Best?
1. "Biography: Theordore Judah," American Experience: Transcontinental Railroad, PBS.org, http://www.pbs.org/wgbh/americanexperience/features/biography/tcrr-judah/

Chapter 3. North Versus South

1. Robert R. Hodges, *American Civil War Railroad Tactics* (New York: Osprey Publishing. 2009), p. 30.
2. The Civil War, "Appomattox Furniture," America's Smithsonian, http://www.150.si.edu/150trav/remember/civil.htm
3. "Native Americans and the Transcontinental Railroad," American Experience: Transcontinental Railroad, PBS.org, http://www.pbs.org/wgbh/americanexperience/features/general-article/tcrr-tribes/

Chapter 4. Finding the Workers

1. "Workers of the Union Pacific Railroad," American Experience: Transcontinental Railroad, PBS.org, http://www.pbs.org/wgbh/americanexperience/features/general-article/tcrr-uprr/
2. David Haward Bain, "Promontory," KUED-7, http://www.kued.org/productions/promontory/interviews/bain.html
3. Milton Meltzer, *Hear that Train Whistle Blow: How the Railroad Changed the World* (New York: Random House, 2005), p. 50.
4. "Chinese Labor on the Central Pacific: 'They Built the Great Wall of China, Didn't They?' " Transcontinental Railroad, Schmoop.com, http://www.shmoop.com/transcontinental-railroad/race.html
5. Sue Seymour, "Transcontinental Railroad," *Promoting Geographic Knowledge Through Literature* Workshop, July 7–19, 2002, http://iga.illinoisstate.edu/literacy%20lps/transcontinental_railroad.htm
6. "Workers of the Central Pacific Railroad," American Experience: Transcontinental Railroad, PBS.org, http://www.pbs.org/wgbh/americanexperience/features/general-article/tcrr-cprr/
7. Walt Whitman, "Songs of Joys," *Leaves of Grass* (New York: Putnam and Sons, 1897), pp. 142–143.
8. Francis Bret Harte, "What the Engines Said," *Yale Book of American Verse* (New Haven, CT: Yale University Press, 1912), and online at Bartleby.com, 1999, http://www.bartleby.com/102/204.html

Chapter 5. On to Promontory Summit!

1. Michael W. Johnson, "Rendezvous at Promontory: A New Look at the Golden Spike Ceremony," Utah State History, http://history.utah.gov/historical_society/educational_resources/lesson_plans/documents/ArticleRendezvousatPromontoryEDITED.pdf
2. "The Harvey Girls: A Slice of American History," HubPages, http://paradise7.hubpages.com/hub/The-Harvey-Girls

Hodges, Robert R. *American Civil War Railroad Tactics.* New York: Osprey Publishing, 2009.

Johnson, Michael W. "Rendezvous at Promontory: A New Look at the Golden Spike Ceremony." Utah State History. http://history.utah.gov/historical_society/educational_resources/lesson_plans/documents/ArticleRendezvousatPromontoryEDITED.pdf

National Park Service: "Golden Spike: Four Special Spikes." http://www.nps.gov/gosp/historyculture/upload/Spikes.pdf

Ross, David, general editor. *The Encyclopedia of Trains & Locomotives.* Berkeley, CA: Thunder Bay Press, 2007.

Schwantes, Carlos and James P. Ronda. *The West the Railroads Made.* Seattle, WA: University of Washington Press, 2008.

Stover, John F. *The Routledge Historical Atlas of the American Railroads.* New York: Routledge, 1999.

Wiatrowski, Claude. *Railroads Across North America.* Minneapolis, MN: Voyageur Press, Minnesota, 2007.

FURTHER READING

On the Internet

Golden Spike National Historic Site, Utah
http://www.nps.gov/gosp/index.htm

Transcontinental Railroad, American Experience, PBS
http://www.pbs.org/wgbh/americanexperience/features/introduction/tcrr-intro/

Harvey Girls, Orange Empire Railway Museums
http://www.oerm.org/pages/Harveygirls.html

Transcontinental Railroad for Kids (Power Point presentations)
http://americanhistory.mrdonn.org/powerpoints/railroads.html

Books

Coleman, Wim and Pat Perrin. *The Transcontinental Railroad and the Great Race to Connect the Nation.* Berkeley Heights, NJ: Myreportlinks.com, 2006.

Evans, Clark J. *The Central Pacific Railroad.* New York: Children's Press, 2007.

Marsh, Carole. *The Transcontinental Railroad: The Big Race to the Golden Spike.* Peachtree City, GA: Gallopade International, 2010.

McNeese, Tim. *The Transcontinental Railroad and Westward Expansion: Chasing the American Frontier.* Berkeley Heights, NJ: Enslow Publishers, 2006.

Meltzer, Hamilton. *Hear that Train Whistle Blow!* New York: Random House Books for Young Readers, 2004.

Sammons, Sandra Wallus. *The Two Henrys: Henry Plant and Henry Flagler and Their Railroads.* Sarasota, FL: Pineapple Press, 2010.

gauge (GAYJ)—The distance between the rails on a railroad track.

locomotive (loh-kuh-MOH-tiv)—A self-propelled vehicle for pulling trains.

maul (MAWL)—A heavy hammer for driving stakes or wedges.

Mormons (MORE-muhnz)—People who belong to the Church of Jesus Christ of Latter-Day Saints.

nitroglycerin (ny-tro-GLIH-suhr-un)—A colorless, thick, explosive liquid.

sabotage (SAH-buh-taj)—Underhanded interference with production or work in a plant, factory, or elsewhere by a wartime enemy.

secede (seh-SEED)—To withdraw from a group, such as from the union of the United States.

transcontinental (TRANZ-kon-tuh-nent-uhl)—Passing or extending across a continent.

trestle (TRESS-uhl)—A framework that supports a bridge or railroad track.

The *General*

Tamra Orr is the author of more than three hundred books for readers of all ages. She graduated from Ball State University in Muncie, Indiana, and writes for many state and national assessment companies. Today, Orr lives in beautiful Portland, Oregon. She and her children and husband ride the Amtrak train from Portland, Oregon, to Seattle, Washington, several times a year and she always takes a moment to appreciate the work it took to create all those miles of rails.